Lanterns

Poems & Prose

By

D h i m a n

Lanterns

Contents

Lanterns

On Heartbreak

Lanterns

You loved them
more than you loved
your own self

and
it still wasn't enough
for them to stay.

Don't be sorry
for giving
all of you to love.

The people
we love the most,
hurt us the deepest.

Some days, no matter how hard you try you miss the person your heart wants. Even if you are in the company of those who fill you with their love, all that your heart craves for is the person that you still love. And the more you try to forget, the more you feel ache in your heart. It feels like the heart only remembers that one person, even if they hurt you, even if they left scars in your heart.

May be
he was in love
with the thought of
loving you.

Lanterns

I shared with you
the parts of me

which I never even
shared with myself before.

Love left us how we began,
broken and complete strangers.

May be all we want
is someone
to hold our heart
with their love
when we are falling apart.

Broken hearts still carry love.

True love stays,
even if you are not perfect.

Some people grow roots inside us

they stay
even when they leave

and I have learned to believe that
sometimes they remain
as long as we exist.

How it all felt right in that moment as if we were meant for each other, as if it was supposed to be perfect like that. But then it all changed, it all fell down like it wasn't strong enough to hold on anymore. We loved each other but we didn't love who we had become. We promised to be there for each other but when we really needed ourselves to be there for us, we weren't there. It hurts me still. It hurts me because I know we were in love but maybe if we loved ourselves a little more, we would have been together a little longer.

Dhiman

Eventually you'll realize
not everything you love
is worthy of a place
in your heart.

Some people will leave you
only to help you realize that
they never loved you at all.

Dhiman

We allow some people
to stay
even when we know
their hearts
have already left.

Lanterns

With all of me
I held you
in my heart
only to see you
move on
and never come back.

And my heart knows
it will never fall for anyone
the way it fell for you.

Lanterns

With you,
I felt the safest.

Sometimes,
the heart remembers
what we so desperately want to forget.

I will always find my way
back to you
and you will always be
the home for me.

You will have my love
even if I don't have you,
even if we don't have us.

Some days, no matter how hard you try you miss the person your heart wants. Even if you are in the company of those who fill you with their love, all that your heart craves for is the person that you still love. And the more you try to forget, the more you feel ache in your heart. It feels like the heart only remembers that one person, even if they hurt you, even if they left scars in your heart.

Some people
leave our life
but they never really
leave our heart.

Lanterns

On Love & Moving on

Lanterns

Be kind to others
but do not forget
to be kind to yourself too.

Give yourself
the love you deserve
over and over again.

It's okay
if they do not give you
the love you deserve
but you will,
you will.

Nothing lasts forever. That means the hardships and the pain you are going through right now won't stay forever either. That means you'll find a way to heal. Remember – life has its seasons, one after another they arrive and leave. You may feel like you won't survive this season of pain and all the struggles you are dealing with. But I assure you, you will. Like the seasons of life your circumstances will change too. And I hope that this period of change makes you realize your inner power, the incredible strength that lies within you.

Your heart
deserves a home
filled with love,
hope and light.

You are
your own reason
to try again, my love.

If the love you lost
didn't take away
a part of your soul,
it wasn't love at all.

Please remember- some people will leave you when you have already given them a place in your heart. The people who could not value you, who promised to stay but never did. In those moments, please remember that those people did not come into your life for you. They came for themselves and they left you for the same reason. It will break you, even make you doubt your worth but it will also help you realize that not everyone you love is deserving of a place in your heart and this will help your heart to prepare itself to choose the right ones. The ones who will make you fall in love with yourself too. *The ones who are really going to stay.*

I hope you find someone
so full of love in their heart
that if this world
ever makes you feel cold again
you will know in your heart
that their love
will keep you warm.

Do not leave yourself
for someone
who didn't come to stay.

Sometimes
all we want
is another heart
willing to listen to our heart

and sometimes
it is all that we need
to keep on going
to believe in who we are.

Love is the greatest freedom. It does not hold you when you are taking flight but encourages you to have faith on your own wings. It reminds you of the strength of your heart. It does not leave you when you fall apart but holds you with warmth until you gather yourself and start again. It is the light that shows you the path of hope when no other light is around. Love trusts you, stays with you for who you are and wants you to be happy and free wherever you are.

Remember:
what loves you truly
will always set you free.

Lanterns

And how it all changes
through the slippery hands of time
like flowers lose their petals
like love loses its way.

Let it go,
not every pain you feel
is yours to carry.

In your journey of life, you'll meet countless people. Most of them will come and eventually leave while some of them will stay. They will not take you for granted or judge you for the person you are. Instead, they will push you to be a better version of yourself. There will be times when you will think of pushing them away but those people will stand by you, holding you with their love, giving you a shelter in their heart, those are the people who deserve to be in your heart and when you find them, please never let them go.

When the right one comes along
you won't have to ask,
he will love you
even on your darkest days
and he will stay.

Your today
doesn't have to follow
the path of your yesterday.

It's not love
if it takes away your happiness
and leaves scars in your heart.
It's not love
if it tells you to be someone else
when all you need is someone
to choose you for who you are.
Love is the comfort, it is the joy
when all things fall apart
love is the strength that holds your heart.

You know it's love
when they are willing to
live inside your heart
and your heart is happy
to be their home.

Love
the way the rain loves the earth,
gently with devotion.

– love is devotion

Love remains even if we don't.

Dhiman

Learn to move on
from the love you lost.

Don't break yourself
for something that is already broken.

Lanterns

On Healing & Self-love

Lanterns

Choose yourself
choose what is best for your heart
and the right people will come
and the love that you deserve, will stay.

In this season of becoming,
be soft with yourself,
your growth may be slow
but you are still growing
and that is what really matters.

Pour all your love into you.

Healing is not perfecting your flaws. It's about embracing them with self-love and assuring your heart everyday that it's okay to be broken sometimes.

It's okay to take time for your healing. You are not here to chase perfection. You are here to learn how to grow freely, to be happy with yourself without judging who you are.

And if the flowers
do not dare to bloom,
then who will?

And when I planted
the roots of my heart
deep in self-love,
I found comfort in walking alone,
I found peace in simply being alive.

Wherever your heart is,
I hope it feels free.

You don't just wake up someday and fall in with yourself. It takes time, it takes patience but more than that it takes self-compassion, empathy and kindness from yourself towards your own heart. you have to be brave enough to forgive yourself, for all the mistakes you have made and all the chances that you didn't take. Like all the other forms of love, you will learn to love yourself by practicing self-love.

You are allowed
to take your time
to grow in your
own beautiful way.

Trust me,
like all the heartbreaks
you have been through,
you will survive this one too.

– you are capable of healing

But when you
fall in love with yourself,
the whole world
falls in love with you too.

Growth is not a one-time choice. It is a lifelong process of choosing to be the best you can be. It means that you are willing to go through the hard days knowing that something better awaits, something that you truly deserve: a life full of joy, peace, love and happiness.

Stay
where your heart
feels easy.

– choices you have to make

Lanterns

May be healing starts
when you realize
this heart is all yours
and you are the one
who has to heal it
with your own love.

It takes time,
this blooming,
this coming back
to your own self.

– patience

Choose happiness, choose peace, choose what makes you fall in love with yourself. Life is too short to spend it on anything else other the things that help your heart grow with love. You don't have to search for it in others, it is already there inside you. Look inside, embrace your heart and be patient. Let selflove be the light and guide of your heart to help you find what you truly deserve.

Dhiman

It takes courage to bloom.

Keep on believing,
the light isn't far away.

Sometimes,
holding onto yourself,
to your own heart,
is what really matters
especially when no else does.

Remember – you don't have to sacrifice who you are to be worthy of love.

You don't have to chase what you already deserve. Believe in your value and have faith in the beauty of your heart. Your right person will find you at the right time.

You are beautiful, worthy
and precious, not because
how you look but because
you are still here, living
this life despite all the
pain and heartbreaks
you have been through.

– you matter because of who you are

Lanterns

I am learning
to fall in love again,
this time
with myself.

I am slowly learning to believe
that I can allow myself to change
and still remain true to who I am.

You don't have to fit yourself in where you feel like an outsider, you really don't. You don't have to go through something you don't feel like worth going through. You deserve happiness and most of all you deserve to be in a place where you are appreciated for who you are, for what your heart holds. You don't have to do anything to make yourself extra worthy in someone else's eyes. Take yourself as you are, who you are. Embrace your heart and all of its love and light. You deserve peace, comfort, love and happiness. Stay where you are needed, valued and loved, where you are allowed to grow in your own way.

Don't look anywhere else,
look inside
everything is inside you.

Lanterns

On Finding Strength & Hope

Lanterns

I hope
whatever it is that you believe
is bigger than all your struggles
I hope
even in this season of change
and uncertainty
you are able to see
how far you have come
from where you began.

I believe in dreams.
I also believe in miracles.

Never forget to appreciate
how much you have grown.

Sometimes being strong means being kind to yourself, being compassionate to your heart and being gentle with your scars. Sometimes it's the courage to embrace your brokenness and not hiding who you are is the truest form of strength.

Dhiman

Let not doubts
rest in your soul
for you are meant
to hold courage
made to carry hope
in your heart
let yourself be as soft
as the first rays of dawn
breathing life on earth
through the gentle hands of light.

Lanterns

Do not hold her
while she blooms
let her grow
in her wildest way.

You don't have to be a star
you can be a candle
and still be the light
in someone else's darkness.

You are so much more than the brokenness you are dealing with and the darkness you are going through.

Dhiman

May you always find a way
to see the light in the world
and have comfort in knowing
that you are not lost,
even if you don't know
where you are.

You are all the magic that you carry in your heart.

Dhiman

Even in the midst of
life's chaos,
you can still find peace
you can still find joy.

You don't change the world by being someone else, you change the world by being you.

Stop looking for your value in someone else's eyes. Look for it in your own heart, in all your beauty and scars. Have faith that you are enough to this wild and beautiful world, just the way you are.

She needed love
but she no longer wished for
another person
to give her
the love she truly deserved
instead she loved herself more
becoming the love of her own.

feel what you need to feel
and then let it go,
do not let it consume you.

You are a gentle drop
of summer rain

carrying mountains
of hope and dreams

like a wildflower
you grow

in a yard filled with
the beauty of your own.

I hope this season of change takes you to the place where you need to be, where your heart will be allowed to grow and free to feel.

Sometimes,
falling can be a new beginning too.

There is love
in her broken pieces
beauty in all her scars.

Dhiman

Sometimes,
holding onto yourself
to your own heart
is what really matters
especially
when no one else does.

One day you'll understand that what you are going through isn't the final chapter of your life. It may be a part of your book but your story is much more than that. Maybe you have lost someone or someone who never loved you back. Maybe you are struggling to believe that you are worthy of love or someone who carries enough value. But one day you'll realize that these are all part of a bigger plan, the plan for your truest life. You may not feel that way right now but when the right moment comes, you'll know it in your heart.

Let this wild and strange world
teach you how to be patient
how to hold your heart
       and how to breathe easy,
for you don't have to know
  or do everything
to be loved
but only to offer yourself kindly
  to this world and move gently
like all the flowers, the stars and the bees.

Lanterns

Even when you are mending
your broken pieces,
you are still growing with grace.

Dhiman

Like

the day

finds its

morning light

you will

find

your

way again.

Lanterns

You will find love
inside you
when you
stop looking for it in others.

And to be alive
in this wild beautiful world
is a privilege indeed.

Lanterns

Even as you feel this way
you are not invisible
you are not unworthy of love
you are here for a purpose
bigger than you know
the path may be dark
and the weight on your shoulder
may be too heavy to carry
but do not be disheartened
and never doubt your worth
for you will find your hope again
in everything that you still have.

You are
an artwork of love,
a light to this universe.

Even in your difficulties you are free to move forward. You are not your weaknesses but all the strength that lies within you. Leave behind what still hurts you. Have the courage to grow in your own way with peace, comfort, selflove and grace.

– You are all the strength breathing in your heart

And I am
always reminded
of my certainty
of my value
when I look for it
not somewhere else
but here
within me.

Lanterns

How gracefully she rises

       even after failing.

Dhiman

You are on your path of
finding who you are
even though you don't know
how long you have to wait
or how far you have to walk
but as you move on at your own pace
through the unknown paths of life
your heart will guide you
and one day you will find your home
have all the love that you deserve
and meet all the people who will stay.

If they aren't helping you grow,
grow alone.

You don't have to be
someone else

to be welcomed by this world
you can be a moth or a bee

and the world will take you
just as you are

as long as you carry inside you
a heart that is free.

And then there is
softness in her heart
and how beautiful and
strong that is.

They don't know what you are going through, even if they pretend to. Your struggles, your pain and all your darkest moments are your own. People might act like they care but the truth is they don't, especially when you face the hardest circumstances of life, when you are down and broken on the inside, when you are struggling to find hope and light. It is in those moments of your journey of life you will get to meet the people who are meant for you, who truly care about you, love you and wants to be there for you. You will also get to realize that no matter happens, you will have your own self always by your side.

Lanterns

She danced
   in her own way
in the rhythm of
   her own song
gently
     aimlessly
         like spring.

You are never too far from yourself,
reach out, offer yourself a helping hand.

Lanterns

To believe
is to rise
is to breathe
is to dream
again and again and again.

Be kind with the person
you are becoming.

Lanterns

And in the end
I hope
I have helped you see
that there is
light inside you too.

Dhiman

Made in the USA
Middletown, DE
13 March 2020